Hatching CHICKS

by Michèle Dufresne

Pioneer Valley Educational Press, Inc.

A mother chicken is called a **hen**.
A hen lays eggs.

A hen sits on her eggs.
This hen is keeping her eggs warm.

This helps the **embryos** inside the eggs to grow. It takes 21 days for chicks to **hatch**.

It is time for the **chicks**
to come out of their eggs.

The baby chicks break out
of the eggs with their beaks.

It was warm inside the eggs.
Now the chicks are wet and cold.

The chicks stay close
to the mother hen to keep warm.

Soon, the chicks' feathers dry.
Now the chicks are soft and yellow.
The soft feathers are called **down**.

Sometimes chicks are hatched in **incubators**. The incubator keeps the eggs warm.

The baby chicks keep on growing.
They grow and grow.
Soon they are chickens!

GLOSSARY

chick: a young chicken

down: soft, fluffy feathers of a young bird

embryo: a young plant or animal before it is complete and able to live on its own

hatch: to break out of an egg

hen: a female chicken

incubator: a warm machine for hatching eggs